# DEVELOPING YOUNG AUTHORS 2-3

## USING FAVORITE LITERATURE TO MODEL GOOD WRITING

W9-ATR-914

**Written by**

Susan Kilpatrick

**Editor:** Carla Hamaguchi
**Illustrator:** Catherine Yuh Rader
**Cover Photographer:** Michael Jarrett
**Cover Illustrator:** Kimberlee Graves
**Designer:** Moonhee Pak
**Cover Designer:** Moonhee Pak
**Art Director:** Tom Cochrane
**Project Director:** Carolea Williams

Thanks to my teaching colleague and good friend, Karla Knott, for sharing her ideas with me.

THE WONDERFUL HAPPENS by Cynthia Rylant, illustrated by Coco Dowley.
Text copyright © 2000 by Cynthia Rylant. Illustrations copyright © 2000 by Coco Dowley.
Used with permission of Simon & Schuster Books for Young Readers, an imprint of Simon & Schuster Children's Publishing.

# Table of Contents

## Writing Lessons Using Literature Models

# Introduction

*Developing Young Authors 2–3* provides over 20 step-by-step lessons that feature a favorite literature selection to model good writing. Each lesson is designed to encourage students to create text innovations. Text innovations are sentences or stories based on the structure of existing text. This type of writing experience will help students gain confidence in their writing, build their vocabulary, develop critical writing skills, and begin to see themselves as young authors. Once this happens, students are ready to tackle more advanced writing assignments such as short narrative writing, responses to literature, and even Writer's Workshop.

Each lesson is based on a familiar children's book. These books were selected because they inspire students in their own writing and serve as models of specific characteristics of good writing, form, and style. The literature selections in *Developing Young Authors 2–3* are grouped in five categories based on which writing skill is most prominently modeled in each book. (Additional writing traits are noted on the first page of each lesson, where appropriate.)

Read the literature selections to the class, and use the discussion and prewriting activities to teach students to recognize familiar writing and the characteristics of good books and to encourage them to make connections between the story and their own experiences. Follow the detailed guidelines to model each text innovation and create a supportive environment where students of all abilities can confidently complete the writing activity. Each lesson includes a reproducible student page and a reproducible book cover. Compile the completed student pages and cover into class or individual books—valuable classroom resources that the student authors will eagerly read again and again.

The lessons in *Developing Young Authors 2–3* enable students to use their prior knowledge and personal experiences to make significant connections with the literature selections. As students begin to make this reading–writing connection, they gradually gain the skills and confidence to write their own stories. Soon students will be on their way toward becoming more proficient writers.

# Benefits of Text Innovation Lessons

Text innovations are sentences or stories based on the structure of existing text. Students create a text innovation by writing their own words or phrases in a sentence frame. The lessons in *Developing Young Authors 2–3* invite students to create text innovations based on the patterns found in familiar children's books. These lessons include the following benefits:

- Students enhance their reading skills by listening to and/or reading the literature.

- Students generate personal writing topics.

- Students begin to make the reading–writing connection.

- Students work with models of good sentence structure.

- Students draw on prior knowledge and experience when they write.

- Students write books that become valuable classroom resources for their classmates to read and reread.

- Students begin to see themselves as authors and gradually gain confidence to write their own stories.

- Students enhance their reading comprehension by reading the text and discussing its meaning.

- Students have many opportunities to build vocabulary as they brainstorm ideas and discuss individual responses.

- Students work toward becoming more proficient at the conventions of writing.

- Students develop listening skills as they listen for the story pattern or the way the author begins and ends sentences.

- Students begin to extend their ideas and add more detail to their writing.

- English language learners and struggling readers and writers receive guided instruction during the reading of the book and the follow-up activity.

# Connections to Reading/Language Arts Standards

Use the activities in *Developing Young Authors 2–3* to help students reach some of your state's required educational expectations. Standards vary by state; the following is a compilation of skills required by many states at the second- and third-grade levels. Check your state standards for more specific information.

## READING

- Students understand the basic features of reading. They select letter patterns and know how to translate them into spoken language by using phonics, syllabication, and word parts. They apply this knowledge to achieve fluent oral and silent reading.

- Students read aloud fluently and accurately and with appropriate intonation and expression.

- Students read aloud narrative and expository text.

- Students read, comprehend, interpret, and evaluate a wide range of materials appropriate to grade level.

- Students listen to and experience a variety of literature.

## WRITING

- Students distinguish between complete and incomplete sentences.

- Students recognize and use the correct word order in written sentences.

- Students write clear and coherent sentences and paragraphs that develop a central idea for a variety of purposes and audiences.

- Students understand and are able to use complete and correct declarative, interrogative, and exclamatory sentences in writing and speaking.

- Students use appropriate conventions of written language, including grammar, spelling, punctuation, language usage, capitalization, and sentence structure.

# Lessons at a Glance

Each literature selection in *Developing Young Authors 2–3* includes a step-by-step lesson that features a whole-class reading and discussion, a prewriting activity, the writing of a student text innovation, and the creation of a class or an individual book. Use the literature selections to introduce, model, and have students practice a writing skill, or use the chart on page 8 to choose a lesson that coordinates with a particular theme or unit of study. The first page of each lesson includes the following information to help you prepare and implement the activities for that book's text innovation.

## LITERATURE SELECTION

Each lesson is based on a familiar children's book. Each book is ideal for reading aloud to the class. Read the brief synopsis to familiarize yourself with the story.

## KEY WRITING SKILL

All fictional literature books possess—to some degree—the basic elements of plot, character, setting, and style. Each literature selection exemplifies and serves as a model of one or more specific writing skills for students to study and then practice in their own writing. This section lists one or more writing skills for you to point out and discuss with students after you read the book to the class. Students will become more proficient writers as they learn to recognize the characteristics of good books and begin to apply this knowledge to their own writing.

## PREWRITING

Most lessons describe a prewriting activity designed to have students brainstorm a list of ideas that they can use to create their text innovation. Record their responses on the chalkboard, or write them on chart paper and post it. The brainstorm list will enhance your print-rich environment as well as validate students' responses, which in turn encourages them to participate in future brainstorm sessions. Add illustrations to the list for less proficient readers and writers. This will serve as a visual clue for students who independently reread the list.

The prewriting activity will encourage students to think about the content of the story they just heard and help them connect it to their own lives through class discussion and brainstorming. This is also a good time to discuss characteristics of the story (e.g., setting, plot), to check for students' reading comprehension by asking them specific questions about the story, and to discuss and define any words students struggled with or did not know.

## WRITING

Each lesson includes one or more reproducible student pages. Read the reproducible pages to the class so students are familiar with the text. Model on the chalkboard or an overhead transparency how to write and complete the frame(s) for each text innovation. Reread the completed sentences with the class. Encourage students to generate their own ideas to complete their text innovations. (Some text innovations do not include end punctuation to accommodate for variations in the length of students' sentences.) If students have difficulty generating ideas, invite them to use the brainstorm list or chart to help them complete their sentence frames. Then, invite them to illustrate their writing.

## MAKING A BOOK

Collect all the completed pages, and combine them in a class book. Make a copy of the reproducible cover. Have a student volunteer color it. Glue the cover to a piece of construction paper, and laminate it. Punch holes through one side of the pages, and bind them with brads, ribbon, or yarn.

Place the completed class books in the classroom library, and invite students to independently read them. Create a special place for these books by decorating a large box or bin. Label the box *Our Class Books*. Students will love reading and rereading these books.

## INVITING OTHERS TO READ AND REVIEW THE BOOKS

Attach a copy of the Reviews reproducible (page 9) to each class-made book. For each book, fill out the first row of the review form by writing the date, your comments about the book, and your signature. (Your comments will serve as a model for others who will fill out the form.) Invite students to take a book home to share with their parents or other family members. Have readers write comments regarding the book on the next blank row of the review form. Ask students to return the books to school. Have other members of the school staff (e.g., principal, nurse, secretary, teachers) read and write a review of the books, too.

# LITERATURE BOOK THEMES

| Title | alphabet | animals | colors | death | decision making | elapsed time | emotions | family | friendship | humor | imagination | letter writing | luck | names | poetry | rhyme | school | self-esteem | superlatives | transportation | whales |
|---|---|---|---|---|---|---|---|---|---|---|---|---|---|---|---|---|---|---|---|---|---|
| The Book of Bad Ideas | | | | | • | | | | | • | | | | | | | | | | | |
| Gina | | | | | | | | | | | | | | | | | | • | | | |
| The Important Book | | | | | | | | | | | | | | | • | | | • | | | |
| Some Things Are Scary | | | | | | | • | | | | | | | | | • | | | | | |
| Today I Feel Silly & Other Moods That Make My Day | | | | | | | • | | | | | | | | | | | | | | |
| Meanwhile | | | | | | | | | | | • | | | | | | | | | | |
| My Teacher's Secret Life | | | | | | | | | | | • | | | | | | • | | | | |
| The Tenth Good Thing About Barney | | • | | • | | | • | | | | | | | | | | | | | | |
| And to Think That I Saw It on Mulberry Street | | | | | | | | | | • | • | | | | | | | | | | |
| Fortunately | | | | | | | | | | | | | • | | | | | | | | |
| Hailstones and Halibut Bones | | | • | | | | | | | | | | | | • | | | | | | |
| I am Really a Princess | | | | | | | | | | • | • | | | | | | | | | | |
| I Go with my Family to Grandma's | | • | | | | | | • | | | | | | | | | | | | • | |
| When I was Young in the Mountains | | • | | | | | | • | | | | | | | | | | | | | |
| The Wonderful Happens | | | | | | • | | | | | | | | | | | | • | | | |
| Chrysanthemum | | | | | | | | | | | | | | • | | | | • | | | |
| What Did I Look Like When I Was a Baby? | | | | | | | | • | | | | | | | | | | | | | |
| A, my name is Alice | • | | | | | | | | | | | | | | | | | | | | |
| Dear Mr. Blueberry | | | | | | | | | | | | • | | | | | | | | | • |
| I'm Like You, You're Like Me | | | | | | | | | • | | | | | | | | | • | | | |
| Things that are most in the world | | | | | | | | | | | • | | | | | | | | • | | |
| Tomorrow's Alphabet | • | | | | | • | | | | | | | | | | | | | | | |

**8**

*Lessons at a Glance*

# Reviews

| Date | Comment(s) | Signature |
|------|-----------|-----------|
|  |  |  |
|  |  |  |
|  |  |  |
|  |  |  |
|  |  |  |
|  |  |  |
|  |  |  |
|  |  |  |
|  |  |  |
|  |  |  |
|  |  |  |

*Developing Young Authors* • 2–3 © 2001 Creative Teaching Press

# Meeting Individual Needs

Often, even the best lessons do not meet the needs of *every* student in the class. The more proficient students finish quickly and get off task, while the less proficient students struggle and do not complete the task. Modify the lessons in this book to meet the needs of every student. Teach the same lesson but offer options such as the ones listed below.

## ENGLISH LANGUAGE LEARNERS AND STRUGGLING LEARNERS

Support these students through the process of writing text innovations by

- meeting with them individually or in a small group to reread the class brainstorm list or chart

- asking them to dictate their chosen responses

- assisting them as they write their responses on their reproducible page

- listening to them read aloud their completed frame or reading it aloud with them

- encouraging them to echo as you read each page

- having them work with cross-age tutors, peers, or parent volunteers

## GIFTED STUDENTS AND ADVANCED LEARNERS

Challenge these students by

- encouraging them to create and use creative ideas that are not listed on the class brainstorm list or chart

- demonstrating the use of descriptive words and expanded phrases to make their sentence(s) more interesting

- inviting them to read aloud their sentence(s) to a partner and listen as a partner reads aloud to them

- inviting them to read their stories to a kindergarten or first-grade class

- providing them with materials to create their own version of the book

# The Book of Bad Ideas

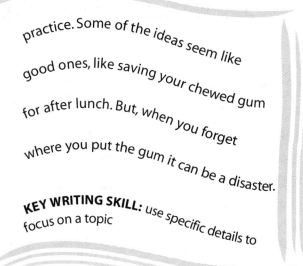

**Laura Huliska-Beith**

LITTLE, BROWN AND COMPANY

This book's list of "bad ideas" shows the sometimes embarrassing, sometimes catastrophic results of putting them into practice. Some of the ideas seem like good ones, like saving your chewed gum for after lunch. But, when you forget where you put the gum it can be a disaster.

**KEY WRITING SKILL:** use specific details to focus on a topic

## Prewriting

Discuss with the class the "bad ideas" mentioned in the book (e.g., #680: letting a friend bring her pet porcupine to your birthday party). Ask students to brainstorm a list of places (e.g., home, dental office) and then a list of bad ideas that they should not do at those places (e.g., jump on the bed, squirt water). Write their responses on the chalkboard or chart paper.

## Writing

❶ Choose a place and a bad idea from the brainstorm lists.

❷ Verbally model your idea for completing the sentence frame. For example, say *Bad Idea #32: At <u>school</u>, it's a bad idea to <u>chew gum in class</u> because <u>it is against the school rules and I could choke on the gum while I'm playing during recess</u>.* Then, write your sentence on the chalkboard or an overhead transparency.

❸ Continue to model other sample sentences, as needed.

❹ Give each student several copies of the reproducible (page 12). Have students generate their own ideas or choose a place and an idea from the brainstorm lists to complete their sentence frames.

❺ Invite students to illustrate their sentences.

❻ Give each student a copy of The Book of Bad Ideas cover (page 13). Have students combine their completed pages and the cover to make a book.

❼ Have students repeat the process to create a book of good ideas (see pages 14–15).

Bad Idea #_____

At _____, it's a bad idea to _____

_____

because _____

_____

_____


Bad Idea #_____

At _____, it's a bad idea to _____

_____

because _____

_____

_____

# The Book of Bad Ideas

Written and illustrated by

_____

We read _The Book of Bad Ideas_ by Laura Huliska-Beith.

Good Idea #_____

At _____, it's a good idea to _____
_____
because _____
_____
_____


Good Idea #_____

At _____, it's a good idea to _____
_____
because _____
_____
_____

Developing Young Authors • 2–3 © 2001 Creative Teaching Press

# The Book of Good Ideas

Written and illustrated by

_____

We read *The Book of Bad Ideas* by Laura Huliska-Beith.

# Gina

## Bernard Waber
HOUGHTON MIFFLIN

Gina moves to an apartment in Queens, New York, where no girls her age live in the neighborhood. At first she's lonely, but she loves sports, and when she shows the boys that she can hit the ball over third base, she becomes part of the crowd. Still, she clings to her dream "of someday seeing other girls play on her team."

**KEY WRITING SKILL:** use specific details to focus on a topic

## Prewriting

Discuss with the class the things that students think will happen on Gina's first day of school. Have students brainstorm things that happened on their first day of school. Record their responses on the chalkboard or chart paper. Discuss with the class sequencing words (e.g., then, finally, later) and how they are used in a story.

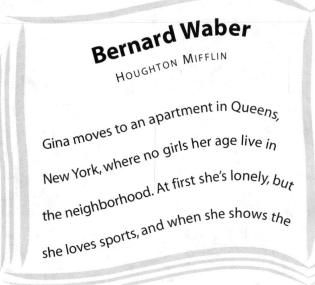

First Day of School

met new friends
wrote a story
played on the playground
wore new clothes
solved math problems

## Writing

❶ Choose ideas from the brainstorm list.

❷ Verbally model your idea for completing the sentence frames. For example say, *On the first day of school, I* met new friends, drew a picture, sang a song, *and* learned a poem. *Then, I* played outside, ate lunch, did a few math problems, *and* read two pages from a book. *Finally, I* wrote down my homework assignment, cleaned my desk, pushed in my chair, *and* said good-bye to my teacher *before I went home. Then, write your sentences on the chalkboard or an overhead transparency.*

❸ Continue to model other sample sentences, as needed.

❹ Give each student a reproducible (page 17). Invite students to generate their own ideas or choose ideas from the brainstorm list to complete the sentence frames.

❺ Encourage students to draw pictures in the border around the text.

❻ Make a copy of The First Day of School cover (page 18). Combine students' completed pages and the cover to make a class book.

On the first day of school,

I _____,

_____,

_____,

and _____.

Then, I _____,

_____,

_____,

and _____.

Finally, I _____,

_____,

_____,

and _____

before I went home.

By_____

*Developing Young Authors* • 2–3 © 2001 Creative Teaching Press

# The First Day of School

Written and illustrated by

_____

We read *Gina* by Bernard Waber.

# The Important Book

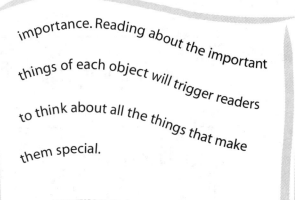

## Margaret Wise Brown
### HarperCollins

Margaret Wise Brown takes a familiar object (e.g., a pencil, the sun, a chair) and describes its many uses to show *its* importance. Reading about the important things of each object will trigger readers to think about all the things that make them special.

**KEY WRITING SKILLS:** use specific details to focus on a topic, use interesting words

## Prewriting

Discuss with the class the things that were "important" in the book (e.g., spoon, daisy, grass). Ask students to brainstorm other objects. Record their responses on the chalkboard or chart paper.

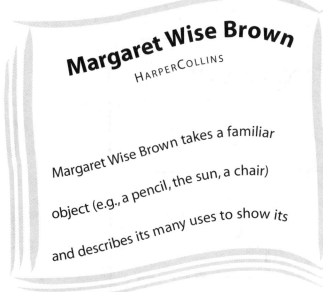

Important Things

a cup
ice cream
the sun
a cow
a pickle

a tree
rain
a car
sand
a watch

## Writing

1. Choose an object from the brainstorm list (e.g., a watch).

2. Think of a reason why that object is important. Verbally model your idea for completing the first sentence frame. For example, say *The important thing about a watch is that it helps you keep track of time*. Then, write your sentence on the chalkboard or an overhead transparency.

3. Model the rest of the sentence frames by stating other important things about the object. For example, say *It is worn on your wrist. It has two "hands." It comes in different shapes and sizes. But the important thing about a watch is that it helps you keep track of time*. Write your sentences on the chalkboard or an overhead transparency.

4. Give each student a reproducible (page 20). Have students generate their own ideas or choose an idea from the brainstorm list to complete the sentence frames.

5. Invite students to draw pictures in the border around the text.

6. Make a copy of the What's Important? cover (page 21). Combine students' completed pages and the cover to make a class book.

The important thing about

_____

is that it _____

_____.

It _____

_____.

It _____

_____.

It _____

_____.

But the important thing about

_____

is that it_____.

By _____

# What's Important?

Written and illustrated by

_____

We read *The Important Book* by Margaret Wise Brown.

*Developing Young Authors • 2–3 © 2001 Creative Teaching Press*

# Some Things Are Scary

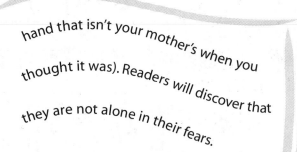

**Florence Parry Heide**

CANDLEWICK PRESS

This compilation of scary things ranges from obvious childhood fears to more abstract ones (e.g., holding someone's hand that isn't your mother's when you thought it was). Readers will discover that they are not alone in their fears.

**KEY WRITING SKILL:** use specific details to focus on a topic

## Prewriting

Discuss with the class the "scary" things that are mentioned in the book (e.g., skating downhill when you haven't learned how to stop). Ask students to brainstorm other scary things. Record their responses on the chalkboard or chart paper.

Scary Things

a monster hiding in your closet

petting an angry crocodile

falling into a volcano

a ferocious lion in your backyard

## Writing

**1** Verbally model your idea for completing the first two sentence frames. For example, say *Thinking about* <u>going on an airplane alone</u> *is scary because* <u>I've never been on an airplane before and I wouldn't have anyone to talk to</u>. *Another reason it is scary is because* <u>when I got off the plane I wouldn't know where to go and I might get lost in the airport</u>. Then, write your sentences on the chalkboard or an overhead transparency.

**2** Then, verbally model your idea for completing the last two sentence frames. For example, say *Seeing* <u>a scary movie</u> *is scary because* <u>there is scary music and scary scenes</u>. *Another reason it is scary is because* <u>I get nightmares after watching them</u>. Then, write your sentences on the chalkboard or an overhead transparency.

**3** Give each student a reproducible (page 23). Have students generate their own ideas or choose ideas from the brainstorm list to complete the sentence frames.

**4** Invite students to illustrate their sentences.

**5** Make a copy of the Some Things Are Scary! cover (page 24). Combine students' completed pages and the cover to make a class book.

Thinking about _____

is scary because _____

_____

_____

Another reason it is scary is because _____

_____

_____

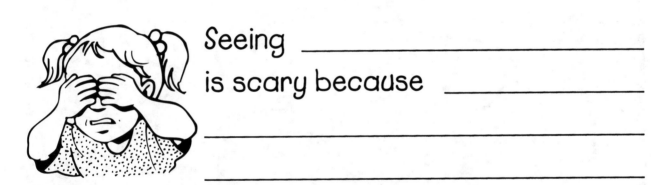

Seeing _____

is scary because _____

_____

_____

Another reason it is scary is because _____

_____

_____

By _____

# Some Things Are Scary!

Written and illustrated by

_____

We read *Some Things Are Scary* by Florence Parry Heide.

*Developing Young Authors • 2–3* © 2001 Creative Teaching Press

# Today I Feel Silly & Other Moods That Make My Day

## Jamie Lee Curtis

HarperCollins

The main character goes through 13 different moods, including silly, grumpy, mean, excited, and confused. This book highlights just about every feeling a young child might have.

**KEY WRITING SKILL:** use specific details to focus on a topic

## Prewriting

Discuss with the class the emotions the character expressed (e.g., happy, angry). Write their responses on the chalkboard or chart paper. Choose an emotion from the list, and ask a student volunteer to role-play that emotion. Discuss the volunteer's actions, and ask students to brainstorm other things that they may do while feeling that emotion. For example, a student may say *When I'm angry, I stomp my feet and shake my arms.*

## Writing

1 Verbally model your idea for completing the sentence frames. For example, say *Today, I feel <u>happy</u> because <u>I have a new baby sister and I saw a rainbow</u>. I am so <u>happy</u> that I <u>will dance to my favorite song and jump in the air with my arms waving and yell "Yippee!"</u>*

2 Give each student a reproducible (page 26). Have students choose an emotion and complete the sentence frames. Encourage students to expand on their sentences by giving examples of why they are feeling that way and what they are doing since they feel that way.

3 Invite students to draw a face showing their emotion to complete the illustration on the reproducible page.

4 Make a copy of the How Do You Feel Today? cover (page 27). Combine students' completed pages and the cover to make a class book.

5 Another option is to give each student several reproducibles. Have students write about a different emotion on each reproducible, and use the completed pages to create an individual book.

Today, I feel _____ because

_____

_____

_____

_____

I am so _____ that I _____

_____

_____

_____

_____

_____

_____

_____

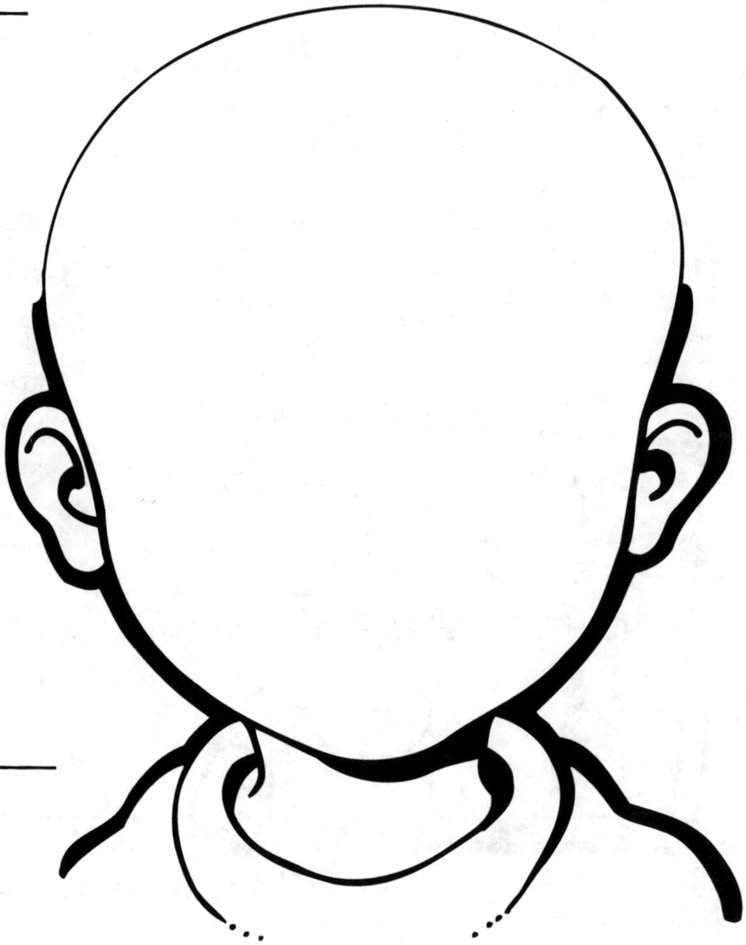

By

_____

*Developing Young Authors • 2–3* © 2001 Creative Teaching Press

# How Do You Feel Today?

Written and illustrated by

_____

We read *Today I Feel Silly & Other Moods That Make My Day* by Jamie Lee Curtis.

*Developing Young Authors • 2–3 © 2001 Creative Teaching Press*

# Meanwhile

## Jules Feiffer

HarperCollins

When Raymond's mom calls him, he ignores her, engrossed in his comic book. As she becomes more insistent, the boy notices a boxed word in the middle of the page: MEANWHILE.... If comic books can use a word to change scenes, why can't he? Raymond writes the word on the wall and is instantly transported to various scenes.

**KEY WRITING SKILL:** develop a setting

## Prewriting

Discuss with the class what "setting" means. Talk about the settings in this story (e.g., pirate ship, outer space). Have students brainstorm a list of interesting places that can serve as a setting for a story. Record their responses on the chalkboard or chart paper. Give each student three pieces of drawing paper. Have students illustrate a different setting on each paper.

## Writing

❶ Give each student three copies of the reproducible (page 29). Invite students to use their illustrations from the prewriting activity to generate descriptive sentences. Have them write a descriptive paragraph about each setting on a separate reproducible. Encourage students to incorporate the three settings together to create a complete story.

❷ Have students fold two 12" x 18" (30.5 cm x 46 cm) pieces of construction paper in half and staple the folded sheets together to create a booklet.

❸ Give each student a copy of the Meanwhile cover (page 30). Invite students to color the cover and glue it on the front of their construction paper booklet.

❹ Ask students to glue one of their completed reproducibles on the first page of the booklet and glue the corresponding illustration on the opposing page. Invite them to glue the rest of their pages and drawings in their booklet.

# Meanwhile . . . .

_____

_____

_____

_____

_____

_____

_____

_____

_____

_____

_____

_____

_____

_____

_____

Written and illustrated by

_____

We read *Meanwhile* by Jules Feiffer.

# My Teacher's Secret Life

## Stephen Krensky
ALADDIN

Everyone knows that teachers live at school. The gym teacher makes the other teachers exercise and dinner is served in the cafeteria. But after a child observes her teacher at the supermarket, at the mall, and even in a park, she begins to think that the teacher has a secret life and wonders when the other teachers will get suspicious.

**KEY WRITING SKILL:** develop a character

## Prewriting

Discuss with the class the things that the child in the book thinks her teacher does after students go home. Have students work with a partner for 10–15 minutes to create a list of things that they think you do when they leave school. Have pairs share their list with the class. Record their responses on the chalkboard or chart paper.

## Writing

1. Choose a few items from the brainstorm list.

2. Verbally model your idea for completing the sentence frames. For example, say *Every day at three o'clock, my teacher* Mrs. Smith *says good-bye to us. I can imagine what happens after we're gone. She* plays basketball on the playground, cooks dinner in the cafeteria, and sharpens all the pencils. Then, write your sentences on the chalkboard or an overhead transparency.

3. Continue to model other sample sentences, as needed.

4. Give each student a reproducible (page 32). Have students choose ideas from their brainstorm list to complete the sentence frames. Encourage students to add descriptive details to expand their sentences.

5. Make a copy of the My Teacher's Secret Life cover (page 33). Combine the students' completed pages and the cover to make a class book.

Every day at _____ o'clock, my teacher _____ says good-bye to us. I can imagine what happens after we're gone. _____
He/She

_____

_____

_____

_____

_____

_____

_____

_____

_____

_____

I know my teacher has a secret life!

By _____

# My Teacher's Secret Life

Written and illustrated by

_____

We read *My Teacher's Secret Life* by Stephen Krensky.

# The Tenth Good Thing About Barney

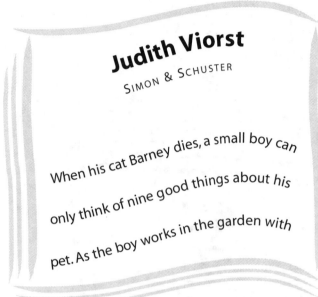

**Judith Viorst**

SIMON & SCHUSTER

When his cat Barney dies, a small boy can only think of nine good things about his pet. As the boy works in the garden with his father, he begins to understand death and finally discovers the tenth good thing about Barney.

**KEY WRITING SKILL:** develop a character

## Prewriting

Discuss with the class the good things the boy in the book listed about his cat (e.g., he was good and brave). Have students sit in a circle, and have each student say one good thing about the person sitting to his or her left. Write students' responses on the chalkboard or chart paper.

is funny
has pretty hair
runs fast
is nice

She is nice.

## Writing

❶ Give each student a reproducible (page 35). Have students choose one person (e.g., mom, friend, grandfather) to write about.

❷ Have students complete the reproducible by writing good things about their person. Encourage them to think of ideas that do not appear on the brainstorm list.

❸ Make a copy of the Good Qualities cover (page 36). Combine students' completed pages and the cover to make a class book.

❹ For an extension, invite students to use the information from their completed reproducible to write a paragraph about their person.

# 9 good things about _____

1. _____
2. _____
3. _____
4. _____
5. _____
6. _____
7. _____
8. _____
9. _____

The **10ᵗʰ** good thing about _____

10. _____

By _____

# Good Qualities

Written and illustrated by

_____

We read *The Tenth Good Thing About Barney* by Judith Viorst.

# And to Think That I Saw It on Mulberry Street

## Dr. Seuss
RANDOM HOUSE

Marco's father has instructed him to keep his eyes open for interesting sights on the way to and from school, but all Marco has seen is a boring old horse and wagon. Imagine if he had something more to report, say, a zebra pulling a blue and gold chariot. Marco tops himself until he is wound up with excitement and bursts into his home to tell his dad what he saw on Mulberry Street.

**KEY WRITING SKILLS:** use descriptive details, use imagination

## Prewriting

Discuss with the class the things the boy imagined seeing on his way home from school. Encourage students to brainstorm things that they can imagine seeing on their own street. Record their responses on the chalkboard or chart paper. Give each student a few pieces of drawing paper. Have students choose two or three items from the list, and invite them to draw pictures of those items. Encourage them to add many details and colors to their pictures.

## Writing

❶ Use a student illustration from the prewriting activity to model the lesson. For example, choose a drawing of a princess sitting on a carpet.

❷ Model how to use the picture as a tool for your writing. For example, look at the picture and say *I saw a beautiful princess in a pink and white dress sitting on a magic carpet.* Then, write your sentence on the chalkboard or an overhead transparency.

❸ Continue to model other sample sentences, as needed.

❹ Give each student a reproducible (page 38). Have students generate sentences based on their pictures. Encourage them to add descriptive details to expand their sentences.

❺ Make a copy of the On My Street cover (page 39). Combine students' completed pages and the cover to make a class book.

# My Street

This is what I saw on my street:

I saw _____

_____

_____

_____

_____

_____

_____

_____

_____

And to think that I saw it

on _____!

By _____

Developing Young Authors • 2–3 © 2001 Creative Teaching Press

# ON MY STREET

Written and illustrated by

_____

We read *And to Think That I Saw It on Mulberry Street* by Dr. Seuss.

# Fortunately

## Remy Charlip

ALADDIN

Fortunately, Ned was invited to a surprise party. Unfortunately, the party was a thousand miles away. Ned's luck turns from good to bad to good again during a series of crazy adventures and narrow escapes.

**KEY WRITING SKILLS:** use descriptive details, use sequence to tell a story

## Prewriting

Discuss with the class the things that happened to Ned on his way to the party. Have students brainstorm various story beginnings for other "Fortunately, Unfortunately" stories. Have students sit on the floor in a circle. Choose one student to start a story by creating a "fortunately" sentence (e.g., *Fortunately, Bob was going to a baseball game*). Then, have the next student say an "unfortunately" sentence (e.g., *Unfortunately, it rained*). Continue the activity until everyone has had a turn creating a sentence. Write student responses on the chalkboard or chart paper. Tell students that they just completed a Fortunately, Unfortunately story.

## Writing

1. Give each student a reproducible (page 41). Encourage students to create their own Fortunately, Unfortunately story by completing the sentence frames.

2. Make a copy of the Our Fortunately, Unfortunately Stories cover (page 42). Combine students' completed pages and the cover to make a class book.

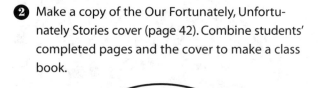

Fortunately, _____

_____ .

Unfortunately, _____

_____ .

Fortunately, _____

_____ .

Unfortunately, _____

_____ .

Fortunately, _____

_____ .

Unfortunately, _____

_____ .

Fortunately, _____

_____ .

Unfortunately, _____

_____ .

Fortunately, _____

_____ .

By _____

# Our Fortunately, Unfortunately Stories

Written and illustrated by

_____

We read *Fortunately* by Remy Charlip.

*Developing Young Authors • 2–3 © 2001 Creative Teaching Press*

# Hailstones and Halibut Bones

## Mary O'Neill

DOUBLEDAY BOOKS

This renowned work of poetry about the colors of the spectrum has become a modern children's classic. This book is a collection of 12 color poems. The descriptive words used in each poem make the readers feel like they can hear, touch, and smell the colors.

**KEY WRITING SKILL:** use descriptive details

## Prewriting

Discuss the poems with the class. Mention how the author uses different senses (sight, sound, taste, touch, and smell) to describe each color. Make a large brainstorm "web" on the chalkboard or chart paper by drawing a circle with five short lines extending from it. Label each line with one of the five senses. At the end of each line, draw a large bubble. Choose a color (e.g., green), and write that color in the center of the circle. Have students brainstorm words that describe green. Write each response in the appropriate bubble. Give each student a piece of paper, and ask students to draw a brainstorm web. Have them choose a color and complete their web for that color.

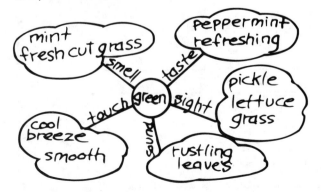

## Writing

❶ Choose a few ideas from the brainstorm web.

❷ Verbally model your idea for completing the sentence frames. For example, say _Green_ is _tall grass and tasty pickles and lettuce_. _Green_ is the sound of _leaves rustling_. _Green_ is the smell of _cool mint_. _Green_ tastes _refreshing like peppermint_. _Green_ feels _like a cool breeze on my face_. _Green is how everything looks during spring._ Then, write your sentences on the chalkboard or an overhead transparency.

❸ Continue to model other sample sentences, as needed.

❹ Give each student a reproducible (page 44). Have students choose ideas from their brainstorm web to complete the sentence frames. Encourage students to add descriptive details to expand their sentences.

❺ Invite students to draw pictures in the border around the text.

❻ Make a copy of the Our Color Poems cover (page 45). Combine the students' completed pages and the cover to make a class book.

_____ is _____

_____ .

_____ is the sound of _____

_____ .

_____ is the smell of _____

_____ .

_____ tastes _____

_____ .

_____ feels _____

_____ .

_____

_____

_____

By _____

*Developing Young Authors • 2–3 © 2001 Creative Teaching Press*

# Our Color Poems

Written and illustrated by

_____

We read *Hailstones and Halibut Bones* by Mary O'Neill.

# I am Really a Princess

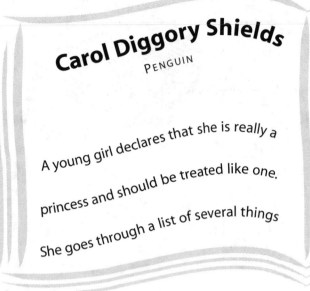

## Carol Diggory Shields
PENGUIN

A young girl declares that she is really a princess and should be treated like one. She goes through a list of several things she should be allowed to do and several things she should not have to do since she is a princess.

**KEY WRITING SKILLS:** use descriptive details, use persuasive writing

## Prewriting

Discuss with the class the things that the princess was not able to do and the things that she thought she should be able to do. Have students pretend they are princes and princesses. Invite them to role-play how they would act. Ask them to tell you some things that they can't do and the reasons why they can't do those things (e.g., *I can't do the dishes because I might get dizzy and faint*). Record their responses on the chalkboard or chart paper. Then, invite students to name things that they should be able to do. Use their responses to create a second brainstorm list.

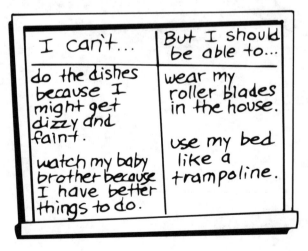

| I can't... | But I should be able to... |
|---|---|
| do the dishes because I might get dizzy and faint. | wear my roller blades in the house. |
| watch my baby brother because I have better things to do. | use my bed like a trampoline. |

## Writing

❶ Verbally model your idea for completing the sentence frames. For example, say *I am a princess! I can't do the dishes because I might get dizzy and faint. But I should be able to wear my roller blades in the house because I am royalty and should be able to do whatever I please.* Then, write your sentences on the chalkboard or an overhead transparency.

❷ Continue to model other sample sentences, as needed.

❸ Give each student a reproducible (page 47). Ask the boys to write *prince* to complete the first sentence frame and girls to write *princess*. Have students generate their own ideas or choose ideas from the brainstorm list to complete the sentence frames. Encourage students to use descriptive details and persuasive writing to explain why they should have the special privileges.

❹ Invite students to illustrate their sentences on the bottom of the reproducible page.

❺ Make a copy of the I am a Prince! I am a Princess! cover (page 48). Combine students' completed pages and the cover to make a class book.

I am a _____! I can't

_____

_____

_____

_____

because _____

_____

_____

But I should be able to _____

_____

_____

because _____

_____

_____

_____

By _____

I am a Prince!

I am a Princess!

Written and illustrated by

_____

We read *I am Really a Princess* by Carol Diggory Shields.

*Developing Young Authors • 2–3* © 2001 Creative Teaching Press

# I Go with my Family to Grandma's

**Riki Levinson**

DUTTON

Dozens of cousins and their families, from all corners of New York, travel to their Grandma's house in Brooklyn for a fun-filled family reunion. Each family arrives by different modes of transportation, everything from a trolley, to a train, to a ferry. The culmination of the group's gathering is a family portrait.

**KEY WRITING SKILLS:** use descriptive details, use repetition

## Prewriting

Discuss with the class the different ways the children and their families in the book traveled to Grandma's (e.g., red and yellow bicycle, dark blue train). Have students brainstorm other modes of transportation and places where they might want to go. Record their responses on the chalkboard or chart paper.

| Ways to travel | Places to go |
|---|---|
| big green bus | cousin's house |
| little red car | park |
| sailboat | mountains |
| airplane | market |

## Writing

1. Verbally model your idea for completing the sentence frames. For example, say *My name is Kim, and I live in Michigan. I go with my family in a little red car to the seashore to feel the cool ocean breeze and soft sand.* Then, write your sentences on the chalkboard or an overhead transparency.

2. Give each student several copies of the reproducible (page 50). Have students generate their own ideas or choose ideas from the brainstorm lists to complete the sentence frames.

3. Have students use a different place and mode of transportation to complete the sentence frames on each page.

4. Give each student a copy of the I Go with My Family cover (page 51). Ask students to draw a picture of their family in the picture frame. Have students combine their completed pages and the cover to make a book.

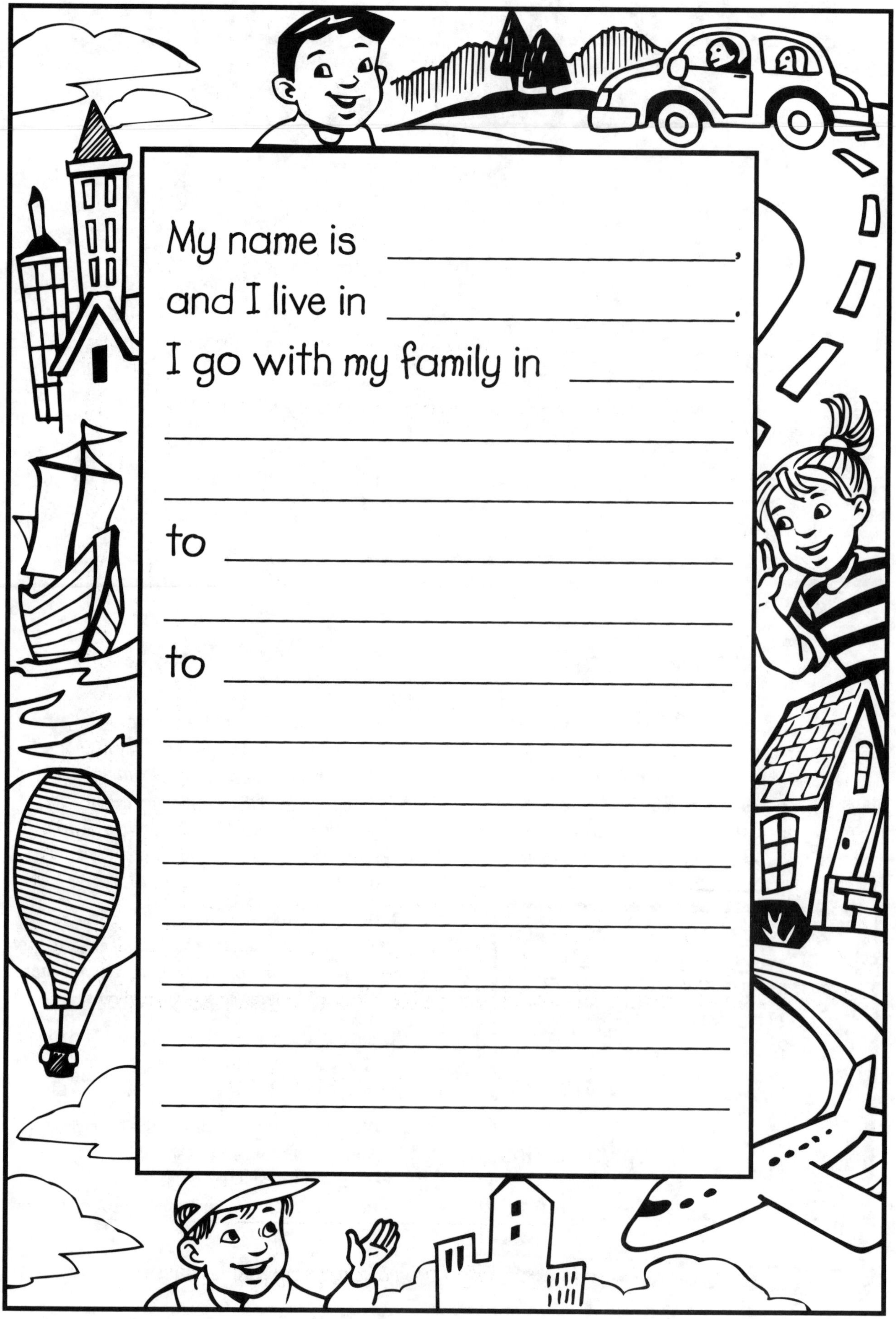

My name is _____,

and I live in _____.

I go with my family in _____

_____

_____

to _____

_____

to _____

_____

_____

_____

_____

_____

_____

_____

*Developing Young Authors • 2–3* © 2001 Creative Teaching Press

# I Go with My Family

My Family

Written and illustrated by

_____

We read *I Go with my Family to Grandma's* by Riki Levinson.

# When I was Young in the Mountains

## Cynthia Rylant

DUTTON

This story about a child's life in the Appalachian Mountains in West Virginia is based on the author's memories of her own happy childhood. It describes what life was like for a child living in a specific setting. The poetic text will inspire students to recall memories of when they were younger.

**KEY WRITING SKILL:** use descriptive details

## Prewriting

In advance, have each student ask family members to tell stories about when he or she was younger. Have students record some of the stories on a piece of paper. Also, encourage students to bring to school photos of when they were younger. Discuss with the class the things the author reflects about when she was a young girl living in the mountains (e.g., Grandmother spread the table with hot corn bread, pinot beans, and fried okra). Have volunteers share their homework assignment and photos with the class.

Crystal

Homework

1. I would go to my grandma's house every summer. She had horses and cows.
2. I learned to swim at the Y.M.C.A. Susie was my swimming instructor.

## Writing

1. Verbally model your idea for completing the sentence frames. For example, say *When I was young in Los Angeles, I walked to school along a busy city street with three of my friends. On our way to school, we would pass my favorite ice-cream shop and my grandmother's pink house. Later, at school we walked through the large wired gate to our classroom. There, we were greeted by Mrs. Jones*. Then, write your sentences on the chalkboard or an overhead transparency.

2. Continue to model other sample sentences, as needed.

3. Give each student a reproducible (page 53). Have students use the information from their homework assignment to complete the sentence frames.

4. Make a copy of the When I was Young ... cover (page 54). Combine students' completed pages and the cover to make a class book.

When I was young in _____,

I _____

_____

_____

_____

Later, _____

_____

_____

_____

_____

By _____

# WHEN I WAS YOUNG . . .

Written and illustrated

_____

We read *When I was Young in the Mountains* by Cynthia Rylant.

# Wonderful Happens

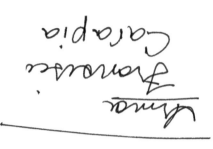

...t

...of the

...d awe into

...nd fresh-

baked bread. The rhythmic text simply describes each object and its origins. This book will encourage readers to appreciate all the wonders of life, including themselves.

**KEY WRITING SKILL:** use descriptive details

## Prewriting

Discuss with the class the objects mentioned in the book (e.g., a rose, a bird, the moon). Discuss the sentence patterns used in the first few pages. Have students work with a partner to create a list of interesting things. Ask students to also list where those things can be found and a few notes on how those things came to be. For example, a student could write that a bird can be found in the blue sky and that the bird hatched from an egg. Invite students to share their lists with the class.

> rainbow — in the sky
> rains, sun shines
> 7 colors
>
> bird — flies, sky
> hatches from
> an egg

## Writing

1. Verbally model your idea for completing the sentence frames. For example, say *In the enormous blue sky shone a beautiful rainbow, wonderful rainbow. The rain came down, the sun shone through, and the wonderful happened: a rainbow.* Then, write your sentences on the chalkboard or an overhead transparency.

2. Continue to model other sample sentences, as needed.

3. Give each student a reproducible (page 56). Have students use their brainstorm list to complete the sentence frames. Encourage them to use descriptive details in their writing.

4. Invite students to draw pictures in the border around the text.

5. Make a copy of The Wonderful Happens cover (page 57). Combine students' completed pages and the cover to make a class book.

In _____
_____,
wonderful _____.

_____,
_____,
and the wonderful happened:

_____

By _____

# The Wonderful Happens

Written and illustrated by

_____

We read *The Wonderful Happens* by Cynthia Rylant.

# Chrysanthemum

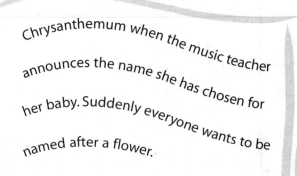

**Kevin Henkes**

MULBERRY BOOKS

Chrysanthemum loves her name until her first day of school when the other children tease her about it. Things change for Chrysanthemum when the music teacher announces the name she has chosen for her baby. Suddenly everyone wants to be named after a flower.

**KEY WRITING SKILL:** use dialogue

## Prewriting

Discuss with the class what Chrysanthemum loved about her name (e.g., the way it sounded when her mother woke her up). Have students share times when they like the way their names sound (e.g., I love the way my name sounds when my friend asks me to play) and the way their names look. Record each set of responses in a separate list on the chalkboard or chart paper.

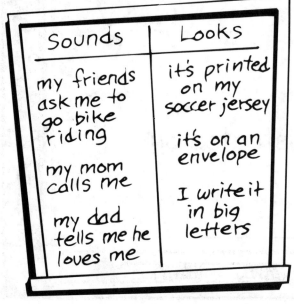

| Sounds | Looks |
|---|---|
| my friends ask me to go bike riding | it's printed on my soccer jersey |
| my mom calls me | it's on an envelope |
| my dad tells me he loves me | I write it in big letters |

## Writing

1. Choose ideas from each brainstorm list.

2. Verbally model your idea for completing the sentence frames. For example, say *I love my name, Mary. I love the way it sounds when my teacher says "Great, job, Mary!" because it makes me feel like I was successful at something. I love the way it looks when it is painted in different colors on a sign on the door of my room because it reminds me that I have a special room all to myself.* Then, write your sentences on the chalkboard or an overhead transparency.

3. Continue to model other sample sentences, as needed.

4. Give each student a copy of the reproducible (page 59). Have students generate their own ideas or choose ideas from the brainstorm list to complete the sentence frames. Encourage them to use descriptive details in their writing.

5. Invite students to illustrate their sentences.

6. Make a copy of the We Love Our Names cover (page 60). Combine students' completed pages and the cover to make a class book.

I love my name, _____.

I love the way it sounds when _____

_____

because _____

_____

I love the way it looks when _____

_____

because _____

_____

# We Love Our Names

Written and illustrated by

_____

We read *Chrysanthemum* by Kevin Henkes.

# What Did I Look Like When I Was a Baby?

## Jeanne Willis
PUTNAM PUBLISHING GROUP

A little boy wonders what he looked like when he was a baby. His mother tells him, "You looked just like your grandpa—bald and wrinkly!" Animals around the world ask their parents the same question and they all are told that they resembled someone in their family, with one exception—the young bullfrog. When he wants to know how he looked as a baby, his mother shows him a picture of a tadpole and he becomes very upset.

**KEY WRITING SKILLS:** use dialogue, use descriptive details

## Prewriting

In advance, ask students to bring from home a baby photo of themselves. Discuss with the class the things the animal mothers said when their babies asked what they looked like. Have students look at their baby picture and list words that describe how they looked. Then, ask students to list things that they did when they were a baby (e.g., slept with a teddy bear, crawled up stairs).

## Writing

❶ Use your own baby picture to verbally model your idea for completing the sentence frame. For example, say *When I was a baby, I was very small. I had brown eyes and a little bit of brown hair that would always stick straight up. I wasn't able to walk then, so I would try to crawl around.*

❷ Give each student a reproducible (page 62). Have students use their brainstorm list to complete the sentence frame. Encourage them to include descriptive details about the way they looked and some things that they would do when they were a baby.

❸ Invite students to illustrate their sentences inside the bib.

❹ Make a copy of the When I Was a Baby ... cover (page 63). Combine students' completed pages and the cover to make a class book.

❺ For a fun extension activity, display all the baby photos on a wall. Read one of the completed reproducibles, and invite the class to guess which photo matches the description. Remind students not to guess when you read their paper.

# When I was a baby, I _____

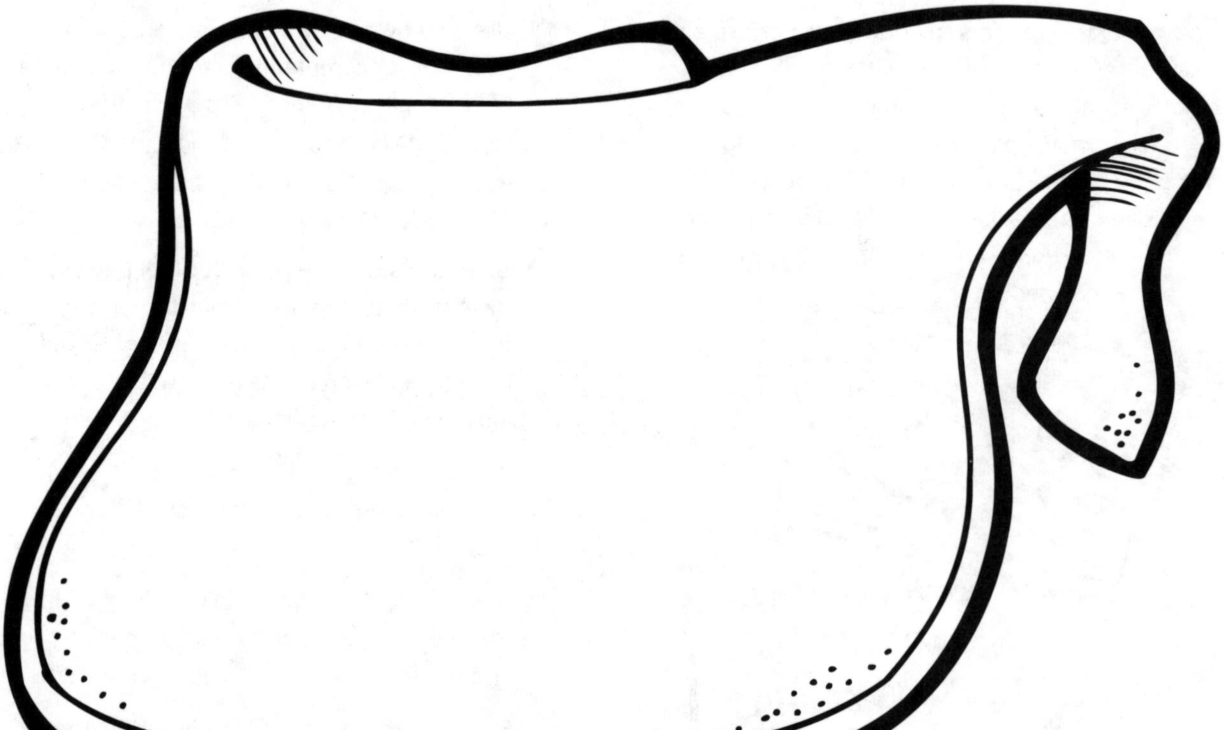

_____

_____

_____

_____

_____

_____

_____

_____

By _____

*Developing Young Authors • 2–3 © 2001 Creative Teaching Press*

# When I Was a Baby . . .

Written and illustrated by

_____

We read *What Did I Look Like When I Was a Baby?* by Jeanne Willis.

# A, my name is Alice

## Jane Bayer

DUTTON

This alphabet book merrily takes readers through the alphabet with this variation of a skipping game. The sequence announces each animal's home and what it is ready to sell. Readers will delight in meeting such characters as Barbara, the bear with balloons for sale in Brazil, and New York Ned, the newt who owns a noodle emporium.

**KEY WRITING SKILL:** use alliteration

# Prewriting

Discuss the pattern of each page of the alphabet book (e.g., My name is Nancy, . . . New York, . . . sell noodles). Divide the class into four groups. Give each group a piece of chart paper and a marker. Assign each group one of the following topics: names, places, foods, or things (e.g., objects, animals, or activities). Have each group brainstorm an alphabetical list for their topic. Invite groups to use a globe, an atlas, a baby name book, or other reference books to help them create their list. Display the lists for students to use as a reference during the writing activity.

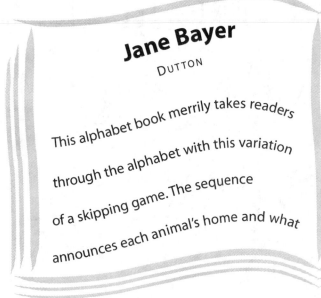

Names
A- Alice, Albert
B- Betsy, Ben
C- Carrie, Carlos
D- Debbie

Places
A - Asia, Australia
B - Brooklyn

Foods
A - apple, artichoke

Things
A- angels
B- boats, books

# Writing

❶ Choose a letter (e.g., *b*) and one item that begins with that letter from the *Names* and *Places* lists (e.g., Betsy, Baltimore). Then, choose three items from the *Foods* and/or *Things* lists (e.g., bread, boats, baseball).

❷ Verbally model your idea for completing the sentence frames. For example, say *B my name is Betsy. I live in Baltimore, and I like bread, boats, and baseball*. Then, write your sentences on the chalkboard or an overhead transparency.

❸ Continue to model other sample sentences, as needed.

❹ Give each student 26 copies of the reproducible (page 65). Invite students to generate their own ideas or choose ideas from the brainstorm lists to complete a reproducible for each letter of the alphabet.

❺ Invite students to illustrate their sentences.

❻ Give each student a copy of the An Alphabet Book cover (page 66). Have students combine their completed pages and the cover to make a book.

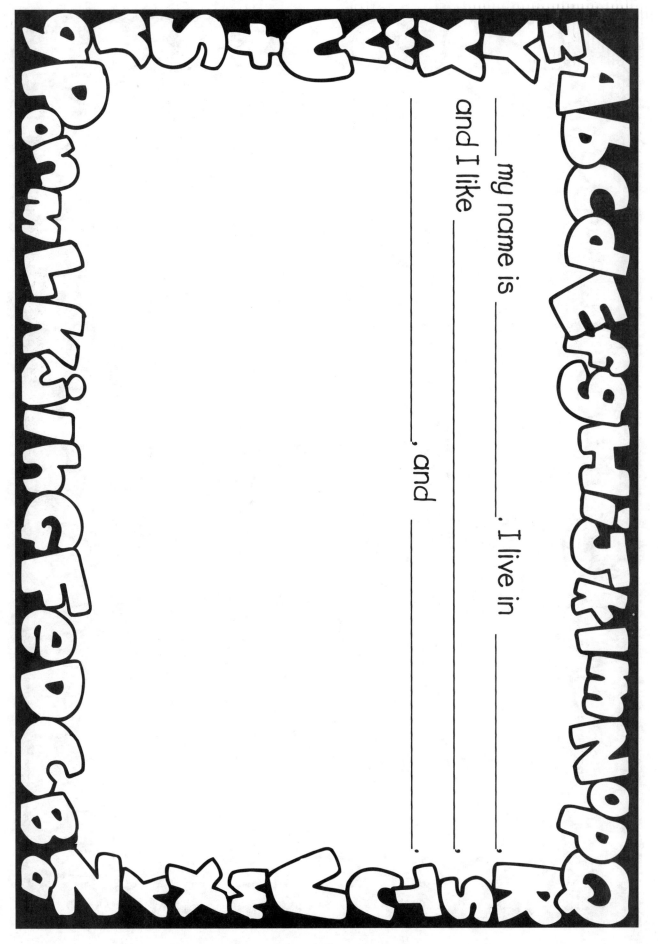

_____, my name is
_____ . I live in
_____ , I live in _____ .
and I like _____
_____ and
_____ .

*Developing Young Authors • 2–3 © 2001 Creative Teaching Press*

An
Alphabet
Book

Written and illustrated by

_____

We read *A, my name is Alice* by Jane Bayer.

*Developing Young Authors • 2–3* © 2001 Creative Teaching Press

# Dear Mr. Blueberry

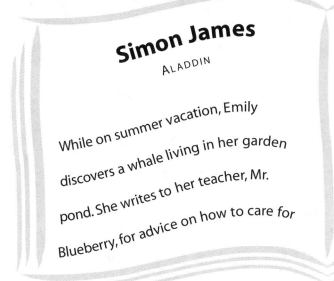

## Simon James

ALADDIN

While on summer vacation, Emily discovers a whale living in her garden pond. She writes to her teacher, Mr. Blueberry, for advice on how to care for her new pet. But Mr. Blueberry responds that she must be mistaken, as whales live in the ocean, not in ponds. In a delightful exchange of letters, Emily learns about whales, and Mr. Blueberry learns about imagination, faith, and friendship.

**KEY WRITING SKILL:** write a letter

## Prewriting

Discuss with the class the format of the book (e.g., letters written between a teacher and child). Talk about the components of a friendly letter (e.g., salutation, body, and closing). Have students brainstorm a list of people they could write a letter to and what types of things they could write about (e.g., ask questions, tell about themselves). Record their responses on the chalkboard or chart paper.

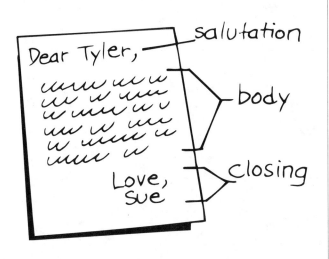

## Writing

1. Verbally model your idea for completing a letter. For example, say *Dear Joey, How are you doing? I'm doing well. Today, I went to the beach and went swimming in the ocean. Have you ever been to the beach? If so, what did you do there?* Then, write your letter on the chalkboard or an overhead transparency.

2. Divide the class into pairs. Give each student several copies of the reproducible (page 68).

3. Have partners write a letter to each other. Encourage students to ask questions in their letter.

4. Ask partners to trade letters, and invite them to correspond by writing another letter. Encourage students to answer the questions that were asked in the initial letter.

5. Have students repeat the process a few times.

6. Give each student a copy of the Dear _____ cover (page 69). Ask students to complete the title by writing the name of their partner on the blank line. Have them combine their corresponding letters and the cover to make a book.

Dear _____,

_____

_____

_____

_____

_____

_____

_____

_____

_____

_____

From,

_____

*Developing Young Authors* • 2–3 © 2001 Creative Teaching Press

# Dear

_____

## Written and illustrated by

_____

We read _Dear Mr. Blueberry_ by Simon James.

# I'm Like You, You're Like Me

## Cindy Gainer

FREE SPIRIT PUBLISHING

Cindy Gainer explores the ways we are alike and how our differences make us unique. In this book, she discusses many aspects of diversity, including features of different ethnic groups, body size, feelings, and cooperation. Readers will discover that even though people are different they can still enjoy spending time together and learning about one another.

**KEY WRITING SKILL:** compare and contrast ideas

## Prewriting

Discuss with the class the ways listed in the book that two people might be alike and ways they might be different. Have students talk about other ways people can be alike and different. Draw a Venn diagram on the chalkboard or chart paper. Label each circle with a different student name. Ask the class how those two students are alike. Write the responses in the intersecting part of the circles. Then, ask how the two students are different. Record each characteristic in the appropriate circle. Give each student a piece of paper. Have students draw a Venn diagram. Ask them to label the circles with their name and a friend's name. Have students complete the diagram by writing the ways they are the same as and different from their friend.

## Writing

❶ Give each student a reproducible (page 71). Have students use the information from their Venn diagram to complete the sentence frames.

❷ Invite students to draw a self-portrait and a picture of their friend in the picture frames.

❸ Make a copy of the Alike and Different cover (page 72). Combine students' completed pages and the cover to make a class book.

_____ and I are friends.

We are alike in many ways. We both _____

_____

_____

_____

_____

We are different from each other, too.

One of us _____

and the other _____.

One of us _____

and the other _____.

By _____

Developing Young Authors • 2–3 © 2001 Creative Teaching Press

*I'm Like You, You're Like Me*

# Alike and Different

Written and illustrated by

_____

We read _I'm Like You, You're Like Me_ by Cindy Gainer.

_Developing Young Authors • 2–3_ © 2001 Creative Teaching Press

# Things that are most in the world

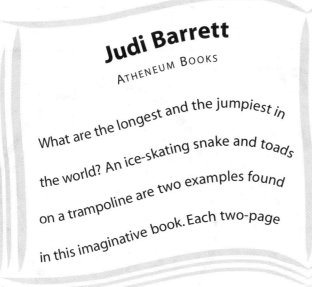

**Judi Barrett**

ATHENEUM BOOKS

What are the longest and the jumpiest in the world? An ice-skating snake and toads on a trampoline are two examples found in this imaginative book. Each two-page spread features an adjective along with a creative idea of what the adjective could be describing. This is a great book to teach students about superlatives.

**KEY WRITING SKILL:** use superlatives

## Prewriting

Discuss with the class the things in the book that were "the most" (e.g., a fire-breathing dragon). Have students brainstorm a few categories (e.g., hottest, silliest, largest). Write each category on a separate piece of chart paper. Then, have students brainstorm a list of things that fit each category. Record each response on the appropriate chart.

## Writing

❶ Choose one of the categories and an item from that category (e.g., the silliest thing and clown).

❷ Verbally model your idea for completing the sentence frame. For example, say *The silliest thing in the world is* _a clown standing on his head while wiggling his feet in the air_.

❸ Continue modeling other sample sentences, as needed.

❹ Give each student a reproducible (page 74). Have students generate their own ideas or choose ideas from the brainstorm list to complete the sentence frames. Encourage them to use descriptive words to expand their sentences.

❺ Invite them to illustrate their sentences in the corresponding balloons.

❻ Make a copy of the Things that are most in the world! cover (page 75). Combine students' completed pages and the cover to make a class book.

The _____ est thing in the world is _____

_____

_____

The _____ est thing in the world is _____

_____

_____

The _____ est thing in the world is _____

_____

_____

The _____ est thing in the world is _____

_____

_____

By _____

*Developing Young Authors • 2–3* © 2001 Creative Teaching Press

# Things that are most in the world!

Written and illustrated by

_____

We read _Things that are most in the world_ by Judi Barrett.

# Tomorrow's Alphabet

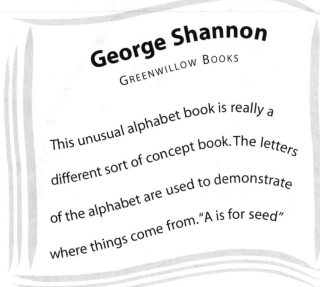

## George Shannon

GREENWILLOW BOOKS

This unusual alphabet book is really a different sort of concept book. The letters of the alphabet are used to demonstrate where things come from. "A is for seed"

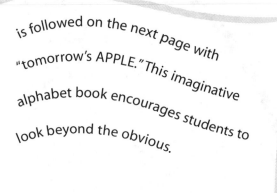

is followed on the next page with "tomorrow's APPLE." This imaginative alphabet book encourages students to look beyond the obvious.

**KEY WRITING SKILL:** use alphabetical format

---

## Prewriting

Discuss with the class the things mentioned in the book. Explain how the first item mentioned does not actually begin with the letter stated but relates to what that item turns into (e.g., "C is for milk—tomorrow's CHEESE"). Have students brainstorm a list of items and then a list of things that those items will become. Record their responses on the chalkboard or chart paper.

B is for cub...
Tomorrow's bear

A is for core...
Yesterday's apple

## Writing

**1** Make 26 copies of the reproducible on page 77 and one copy of the Tomorrow's Alphabet cover (page 78) for each student. Combine the pages to create a booklet. Give each student a booklet.

**2** Have students generate their own ideas or choose ideas from the brainstorm lists to complete each sentence frame.

**3** Invite students to illustrate each sentence.

**4** For an extension, give each student a booklet with 26 copies of the reproducible on page 79 and one copy of the Yesterday's Alphabet cover (page 80). Challenge students to create a "Yesterday's Alphabet Book." For example, students could write _A is for core—yesterday's apple_ or _B is for man—yesterday's boy_.

_____ is for _____ —

tomorrow's _____

# TOMORROW'S ALPHABET

Written and illustrated by

_____

We read *Tomorrow's Alphabet* by George Shannon.

_____ is for _____ —

yesterday's _____

Written and illustrated by

_____

We read *Tomorrow's Alphabet* by George Shannon.

*Developing Young Authors • 2–3 © 2001 Creative Teaching Press*